F.O.G.
FOCUS ON GOD

But seek first the kingdom of God and His righteousness, and all these things shall be added to you.
— Matthew 6:33 (NKJV)

Trilogy Christian Publishers

A Wholly Owned Subsidiary of Trinity Broadcasting Network

2442 Michelle Drive

Tustin, CA 92780

Copyright © 2024 by Gail Charles Wright

Unless otherwise noted, scriptures are taken from the New King James Version®. Copyright © 1982 by Thomas Nelson. Used by permission. All rights reserved.

Complete Jewish Bible (CJB) copyright 1998 by David H. Stern. Published by Jewish New Testament Publications Inc. All rights reserved.

Scripture quotations marked (KJV) are taken from The Holy Bible, King James Version. Cambridge Edition: 1769.

All rights reserved, including the right to reproduce this book or portions thereof in any form whatsoever.

For information, address Trilogy Christian Publishing

Rights Department, 2442 Michelle Drive, Tustin, CA 92780.

Trilogy Christian Publishing/ TBN and colophon are trademarks of Trinity Broadcasting Network.

For information about special discounts for bulk purchases, please contact Trilogy Christian Publishing.

Trilogy Disclaimer: The views and content expressed in this book are those of the author and may not necessarily reflect the views and doctrine of Trilogy Christian Publishing or the Trinity Broadcasting Network.

10 9 8 7 6 5 4 3 2 1

Library of Congress Cataloging-in-Publication Data is available.

ISBN 979-8-89597-048-5

ISBN (ebook) 979-8-89597-049-2

F.O.G.
FOCUS ON GOD

But seek first the kingdom of God and His righteousness, and all these things shall be added to you.
— Matthew 6:33 (NKJV)

GAIL CHARLES WRIGHT

Dedication

I dedicate this book to my parents, who have transitioned to heaven; they planted seeds of faith and taught us to love and seek the Lord daily. I also would like to honor all those pastors who have poured into my life, especially those that have transitioned to heaven and are cheering us on—Rev. Dr. Frederick K.C. Price, Pastor Jack Hayford, Dr. Charles Stanley, and Pastor Jim Cobrae. I am deeply thankful for the generals of faith who continue to pour into my life: Kenneth Copeland, Gloria Copeland, Keith Moore, Jesse Duplantis, Brother Jerry Savelle, Sister Billye Brim, Andrew Wommack, Larry and Tiz Huch, and my pastors—George Pearson and Terri Copeland Pearson.

Foreword

By Gail Charles Wright

On a daily basis you will have several things competing for your attention. This 21-day devotional will help you grow closer to God when you F.O.G.—Focus on God! When you focus on God you are blessed with the favor of God. I invite you to spend quality time with the Lord. Don't rush as you meditate on His Word. Meditating on His Word helps you to renew your mind. As a benefit, He has promised that as you draw closer to Him He will draw close to you (James 4:8—New King James Version)!

F.O.G. FOCUS ON GOD

But seek first the kingdom of God and His righteousness, and all these things shall be added to you.
— Matthew 6:33

— TABLE OF CONTENTS —

Part 1:
F.O.G.—Godly Wisdom vs. Worldly Knowledge..... 13
   Day 1: Seeking the Face of God 15
   Day 2: The Benefits of Godly Wisdom 19
   Day 3: Godly Wisdom Brings Favor of God 23
   Day 4: Handling Temptations 27
   Day 5: Flight or Fight 31
   Day 6: Pride Blocks Your Blessing 39
   Day 7: Walking in Love 43

Part 2:
F.O.G.—Developing Godly Relationships 47
   Day 8: Developing Relationships that Honor God . 49
   Day 9: Addressing Moral Impurity 53
   Day 10: Movies, Music, and Messages 57
   Day 11: Eliminating Bitterness and Strife 61
   Day 12: Write the Vision: Developing Godly Plans 65
   Day 13: Honoring Parents 69
   Day 14: Honoring Those in Authority 73

Part 3:
F.O.G.—God's Purpose for Your Life 77
   Day 15: Develop Your God-Given Gifts and Talents 79
   Day 16: What Is God's Plan for Your Life? 83
   Day 17: Applying God's Wisdom for Your Future 87
   Day 18: Choosing Godly Business Associates 91
   Day 19: Wisdom for Trials and Tests 95
   Day 20: Success God's Way 99
   Day 21: Establishing a Close Relationship with God 103
Psalm 91 106
Closing Prayer 111

Epilogue..	113
About the Author	115
Resources for Further Growth & Development	116
Prayer of Salvation/Receive the Holy Spirit..................	117

— PART 1 —
Godly Wisdom vs. Worldly Knowledge

INTRODUCTION:

Everyone wants to be a success in life. No child, when asked what you want to be when you grow up, desires to be a failure. Most of us try to accomplish this with education, networking, family contacts, and other worldly means. F.O.G. - focus on God will help you obtain a closer relationship with God. If you have never made God the Lord of your life, we can take care of this so that you will have everything that God desires for you and it will help when you "seek first the kingdom of God, His righteousness, and all these things [e.g. health, needs met, home, car, college tuition paid, etc.] shall be added to you."

Before we venture any further, if you have not made Jesus the Lord of your life, I invite you to pray this prayer, say out loud:

"Dear Lord Jesus, I believe You died for me and rose again on the third day.

I believe You are the Son of God. I confess I am a sinner and that You died for my sins.

I need Your love and forgiveness. Please forgive me for all my

sins. I ask You to come into my heart and be my Savior and Lord of my life. Thank You for coming into my heart and making me a child of God."
Amen

If you prayed the above prayer, congratulations! Welcome to the body of Christ!

F.O.G. is a 21-day devotional that will help you grow closer with God. This devotional will help teens, college students, and adults spend more time with God and develop a relationship with Him. The stories shared reflect the trials and challenges faced by family, friends, and colleagues. We are losing our teens and young adults to the world. Satan is working overtime on drawing them from God and to the world. Satan is making inroads via the internet, TV, video games, movies, music, friends, and ungodly "educational influences." There is a battle raging for our families, children, teens, and young adults; F.O.G. is one of many tools designed to break the forces of darkness as you draw closer to our Lord through "focusing on God!"

DAY 1 — Seeking the Face of God
Proverbs 1

If you desire to be successful in all areas of your life, you must F.O.G.—focus on God and not on the world.

The book of Proverbs is rich with wisdom relative to spiritual, physical, and financial success. Proverbs 1 warns us against rejecting Godly wisdom. When we reject Godly wisdom, we suffer the consequences and then wonder where God is. The Book of Proverbs was written that we may obtain Godly wisdom and instruction on how to live our lives.

Mary, as a child, attended vacation Bible school every summer. During the summer of 2022, at the age of six, she accepted Jesus Christ as her Lord and was baptized. Mary learned at an early age to seek the face of God and to pray about everything. Mary was nervous about her sixth grade geography project at school; each student was assigned a state and Mary was given the state of Maryland as her assignment. One of the tasks was to prepare a tri-fold display board for her particular state. She wanted to do her best on the project because of the percentage of points this project would count toward to her final grade. Many of Mary's friends in her class were only doing routine research and she was encouraged to do the same. At lunchtime, Mary's friends shared how they were going to research their particular states on the internet and paste the facts onto their display. They encouraged Mary to do the same, since it was only one project. However, her parents encouraged her to seek God, pray, and ask the Lord for guidance about how to approach the project. Mary and her parents routinely prayed as a family daily and prayed over the school assignment, asking the Lord to guide her steps. She was led by the Lord to write a letter to the governor of Maryland and share with him about her school project. Mary was so excited when she received a package in the mail from the governor of Maryland. Mary was the only student in her class that had a letter from the governor of her assigned state, which she proudly placed on her display. In addition, the governor sent her the state pin and shared other interesting facts about the state of Maryland that she was able to relate during the oral project presentation time. Mary was so excited and thankful for the godly wisdom of her parents and guidance from the Lord which helped her earn a grade of 95 on her class assignment.

Proverbs 1:29-33

When you choose to accept worldly knowledge and walk after the flesh you will reap the rewards of those decisions. As a reminder, we are in the world but not of this world.

Focus on God, seeking first God with all your heart and developing a close relationship with Him as your Father. Many of us try to find wisdom in books and by searching the internet and social media platforms. We are not suffering from a lack of knowledge in this technology world; we are suffering from a lack of godly wisdom! Focus on God and ask Him for wisdom for every issue you may encounter—the Holy Spirit will lead and guide you. God is concerned and cares about those things which concern you.

F.O.G. INSPIRATION

List at least three areas in your life where you need to apply godly wisdom:

1. _____
2. _____
3. _____

F.O.G. PRAYER

Father, Your Word says in James 1:5 if any one lack wisdom, let him ask of God, that giveth to all men liberally and without reproach, and it shall be given to him or her. I am asking for Your wisdom and believe that I will daily increase in Your wisdom and understanding, in Jesus' name I pray. Amen!

DAY 2 — The Benefits of Godly Wisdom

Proverbs 2 challenges us to actively seek skillful and godly wisdom. Focus on God: in Proverbs 2:6 King Solomon writes—"For the Lord gives wisdom; from His mouth comes knowledge and understanding." If you desire to be protected, seek godly wisdom. Proverbs 2:7 tells us that God hides away sound and Godly wisdom and stores it for the righteous; He is a shield to those who walk uprightly and in integrity.

Amy loved to play volleyball and tried out for her high school team; she was excited when she was selected. She was a skilled player and received a college scholarship. She believed it was an answer to prayer and was excited about playing collegiate volleyball. When she arrived at college she was surprised that she was only black player on the team, and tried her best to fit in. The other team members appeared to welcome her; however, she noticed that she was not invited to any gatherings that were not team related. She felt isolated and alone. During practice and at their games, the other team members were friendly and welcoming to Amy. Amy continued to practice and focus on her studies. This was different from high school and she had to apply herself. Amy's skills as a player were recognized by their coach and she was nominated as Outstanding Freshman Player of the Year. The other team players did not celebrate Amy's achievements and the isolation became more intense. Amy would spend her time alone, praying about what was happening and seeking the Lord's guidance. As a member of the team there were guidelines that all of the team members had to conduct themselves by: no drugs or alcohol and compliance with the team curfew. Several of her team members decided to drive to a nearby party at another college in the area. They knew that Amy did not drink and decided to ask Amy to come along so that she could be the designated driver. However, Amy decided against going, which really upset the other team players. Amy later found out that the four girls were pulled over by local police officers for driving under the influence. All the girls in the car were issued warnings and the driver was issued a citation for driving under the influence; this was a violation of her scholarship and it was revoked. Amy realized that while she was being isolated, she was being protected and covered by the prayers of her parents and her spending time with Lord.

Today's world confuses godly wisdom with knowledge and worldly acceptance. Wisdom does not come from years of experience or from books. It comes from a focus on God. As you spend time growing in your relationship with God, you are growing in His wisdom. His wisdom can be applied daily to all areas of your life: "Which college should I apply to?" "Should I go to college?" "Should I date Paul?" "Should I date David?" "Should I apply for a job at company XYZ?" "Should I focus on company ABC?" God is concerned about daily things that concern you and desires to help and guide you.

When you spend time focusing on God you can be expected to be blessed with prosperity, daily provision and protection. In Proverbs 2:7 King Solomon tells us that God will be a shield to you as you walk uprightly before him. We are promised divine protection and guidance.

F.O.G. INSPIRATION

Can you think of a time recently when you did not use godly wisdom? What was the outcome?

_____
_____
_____
_____

What can you do to ensure that your decisions are founded on God's Word?

_____
_____
_____
_____

F.O.G. PRAYER

Father, I purpose in my heart to daily seek and apply Your wisdom. I need the Holy Spirit to lead and guide. Father, Your Word says in James 1:5 "If any of you lack wisdom, let him ask of God who gives to all men liberally and without reproach, and it will be given to him." I am asking for Your wisdom and that You help me to honor You in all that I do. In Jesus' name I pray. Amen!

DAY 3 — Godly Wisdom Brings Favor of God

The majority of us have spent time trying to impress others to gain favor and other worldly recognition. We never focus on the fact that our gifts and other talents were given to us by our Heavenly Father to honor Him. So why are we so desperate to obtain favor of man and seek to please him. In Proverbs 24:1 NKJV, King Solomon tell us "Do not be envious of evil men, nor desire to be with them."

Angel was gifted with a beautiful singing voice and was very active in her church's choir. Angel loved the Lord and enjoyed serving Him by singing in the choir. Seeking to be popular at school, Angel started hanging out with others who did not share her beliefs and began to draw her away from the church. These new friends encouraged her to use her talent to make money because singing in the church choir doesn't pay. Angel loved the attention and the money she began making as a background singer on demo tapes for various inspiring artists. Angel's new friends earned enough money to buy expensive new cell phones, laptops, and designer clothing. Angel desired to be more like them; she stopped singing in the choir and only went to church once a month versus weekly as she had done previously. She was told that this would be her big break into the music business. What Angel did not realize was her new friends were constantly looking for new singers and constantly recruiting other talented young singers to use and then drop. Her parents and friends at church noticed the change in her behavior and warned her. Angel's father encouraged her to pray about her decisions and whether her new friends were real friends.

Angel noticed new singers joining the group and soon she was no longer in demand. Her new friends soon stopped responding to her calls or text messages. The group changed the location of recording sessions and all communication with Angel was blocked. Angel felt isolated and used; she felt betrayed. Angel's parents continued praying for her and she eventually returned to church and started back singing in the choir. Her parents and friends in the choir encouraged her to focus on God and not on what she thought she had lost. Angel was asked by a visiting Christian group to join them during the summer as one of their background singers. This, she realized, was only the favor of God because she was seeking Him first and not the world!

The book of Proverbs tells us very clearly that Godly wisdom brings Favor of God and man.

In Proverbs 8:35 (KV) King Solomon tells us, "For whoso findeth me findeth life, and shall obtain favour of God and man." Proverbs 3:4 (KJ V) states, "So shalt thou find favour and good understanding in the sight of God and man."

God's Word promises that the Lord will bless the righteous with favor and compass him as with a shield. Godly choices bring protection, blessing, and favor.

F.O.G. INSPIRATION

Think of a time when you envied someone you knew did not share your Christian beliefs and morals; why did you feel that way?

_____
_____
_____
_____

Why do you think God wants to bless you with favor?

_____
_____
_____
_____

F.O.G. PRAYER

Father, thank You for the gifts and talents that You have given to me. May I use them to bring You honor and glory. Lord, I ask that You reveal to me any demonic spirits masquerading as a friend and that they be speedily removed from my life. I seek Your favor and not the favor of man, and I am so grateful that I have this promise: that Your favor shall surround me as a shield.

DAY 4 — Handling Temptations

We all have or will experience temptations in our lives. It is important to realize who the author of your temptation is. God does not tempt us to do evil, and the Holy Spirit, your helper, will help you to withstand evil.

Harold, a sophomore in college, had an English literature term paper due. Harold had started his research but was constantly drawn away from studying by his roommate, Edward. Edward was a party person who enjoyed staying out late and was failing three of his four classes. If they were not out having a good time, they were playing video games several hours a day. Edward was a bad influence on Harold, but they had been friends since elementary school and had always planned on attending the same college and living together. Harold's parents were concerned about Harold's grades and were always encouraging him to put God first and recommending that he pray about everything, including his study habits and living situation. Harold was being influenced by his roommate and was rebellious toward his parent's' guidance.

Harold thought that he had time to complete his assignment; however, before he realized it, his term paper deadline was less than 48 hours away. With his work schedule, Harold did not know how he was going to get it done. Edward suggested to Harold that he purchase a paper or hire another student to write the paper for him. Edward shared this was what he did and had never had any problems with his professors accepting the work as his. Edward gave Harold the phone number of a student that he had used to write a paper for him and bragged that he received an "A" on the assignment. Harold was torn and confused about what to do; should he take the easy way out and hire someone to write the paper for him or take time off from his job and write the paper himself? Harold decided to take the easy way out and hired the student to write the paper for him. Harold turned in the paper and received a failing grade. The professor scheduled a meeting with Harold and revealed that Harold had received a failing grade because the paper had previously been submitted by another student. Harold was accused of plagiarizing another student's work.

F.O.G. INSPIRATION

In Psalms 1:1-2 (NKJV) God said:

Blessed is the man who walks not in the counsel of the ungodly, Nor stands in the path of sinners, Nor sits in the seat of the scornful But his delight is in the law of the Lord; and in His law he meditates day and night.

Do you think Harold received godly counsel from his roommate? Why do you think Harold accepted the counsel of his roommate versus the counsel of his parents?

_____
_____
_____
_____

Read Psalm 1. What does the Psalm 1 say about the wicked?

_____
_____
_____

What does Psalm 1 say about the man or woman that delights in the Lord?

_____
_____
_____
_____

Do you recall a time when you were tempted to do something unethical? Read Proverbs 24:1-6. What does the word of God say about evil men? List three benefits of godly wisdom:
1. _____
2. _____
3. _____

F.O.G. PRAYER

Father, I ask for godly wisdom to handle any temptation that I may encounter today. Your Word says that if anyone lacks wisdom to ask; I am asking and seeking Your wisdom. I purpose in my heart to lean not unto my own understanding but only trust in You and believe that You have heard and answered my prayer. In Jesus' name I pray. Amen!

DAY 5 — Flight or Fight

Sheila, because of her parents' deployment, was attending her third new school in the past two years. She was excited about going to middle school and looked forward to changing classes and making new friends. Sheila was very petite for her age and looked only about eight years old compared to other girls in middle school. She was constantly picked on due to her appearance and her new braces. Daily, she became the target of the school bully. Becky was 5 foot 8 inches tall and pushed her weight around at school. The school's administrator was aware of her behavior but elected to do nothing since her father was a military MP. It was a known fact around the school that Becky's parents condoned her behavior. Every day Becky pushed Sheila around in the hallway. It was like David and Goliath. Sheila told her parents about what was happening at school and her parents contacted the school administrator, who failed to address the problem. Sheila's parents also contacted her school teacher and asked for help, who only referred them back to the school administrators, who failed to address the problem.

Sheila had become fearful of Becky and tried her best to avoid her. The only relief she had was on the weekends when school was closed. Becky's behavior became increasingly more aggressive and she started shoving Sheila into the lockers in the hallway. Becky posted on her Facebook page that she was going to attack Sheila after school. Sheila decided to take the abuse and prayed for help. Sheila finally became tired of the abuse, feared for her safety, and was forced to defend herself. Once she confronted Becky, the abuse stopped.

Sheila's situation ended when she decided to stand up to the bully in her school. However, not all bullying situations have a favorable ending. Many U.S. children have experienced bullying, whether online or in person. Some parents have turned to home-schooling or other measures to prevent bullying.

The U.S. Centers for Disease Control and Prevention's Youth Risk Behavior Survey found that around 20 percent of high school students reported being bullied at school in its biennial surveys between 2011 and 2020, dropping to 15 percent in 2021. The percentage of teens reporting that they had been cyberbullied remained mostly flat between 2011 and 2021.

Bullying is a major concern for parents as well as educators. A Pew Research Center survey of parents conducted in the fall of 2022 found that nearly three-quarters of parents said they were either very or somewhat concerned about their child being bullied, up from 60 percent in 2015.

BULLYING STATISTICS (SOURCE: STOPBULLYING.GOV)

Here are federal statistics about bullying in the United States. Data sources include the Indicators of School Crime and Safety: 2019 (National Center for Education Statistics and Bureau of Justice) and the 2017 Youth Risk Behavior Surveillance System (Centers for Disease Control and Prevention).

HOW COMMON IS BULLYING?

- About 20% of students ages 12-18 experienced bullying nationwide.

- Students ages 12–18 who reported being bullied said they thought those who bullied them:

  § Had the ability to influence other students' perception of them (56%).

  § Had more social influence (50%).

  § Were physically stronger or larger (40%).

  § Had more money (31%).

BULLYING IN SCHOOLS

- Nationwide, 19% of students in grades 9–12 report being bullied on school property in the 12 months prior to the survey.

- The following percentages of students ages 12-18 had experienced bullying in various places at school:

  § Hallway or stairwell (43.4%)

  § Classroom (42.1%)

  § Cafeteria (26.8%)

  § Outside on school grounds (21.9%)

  § Online or text (15.3%)

  § Bathroom or locker room (12.1%)

  § Somewhere else in the school building (2.1%)

- Approximately 46% of students ages 12-18 who were bullied during the school year notified an adult at school about the bullying.

CYBERBULLYING
- Among students ages 12-18 who reported being bullied at school during the school year, 15% were bullied online or by text.
- An estimated 14.9% of high school students were electronically bullied in the 12 months prior to the survey.

TYPES OF BULLYING
- Students ages 12-18 experienced various types of bullying, including:

    § Being the subject of rumors or lies (13.4%)

    § Being made fun of, called names, or insulted (13.0%)

    § Pushed, shoved, tripped, or spit on (5.3%)

    § Left out/excluded (5.2%)

    § Threatened with harm (3.9%)

    § Others tried to make them do things they did not want to do (1.9%)

    § Property was destroyed on purpose (1.4%)

Bullying victims are between two and nine times more likely to consider suicide than non-victims, per a study performed by Yale University. Ten- to fourteen-year-old girls have a higher risk of suicide per the study findings. Researchers have identified three types of bullying:

- Physical Bullying
- Verbal Bullying
- Social Bullying

F.O.G. Inspiration

In Psalm 121: 7-8 (NKJV) God said:

> *"The Lord shall preserve you from all evil; He shall preserve your soul. The Lord shall preserve your going out and your coming in from this time forth, and even forevermore."*

Has the Lord ever protected you or a family member from evil?

_____
_____
_____
_____

What do you think Sheila should have done? Defend herself and fight, and as a Christian prayed for the bullies at her school?

_____
_____
_____
_____

— F.O.G. | FOCUS ON GOD —

In Proverbs 20:3 (KJV) King Solomon states:

"It is an honour for a man to cease from strife: but every fool will be meddling."

Bullying is a serious problem that requires godly wisdom. What can you do to help prevent or address bullying?

_____
_____
_____
_____

Do you know someone who is being bullied at school? Is there anything you can you do to help?

_____
_____
_____
_____

Have you experienced cyberbullying? What can you do to stop or prevent cyberbullying?

_____
_____
_____
_____

— GAIL CHARLES WRIGHT —

F.O.G. Prayer

Heavenly Father, I thank You for Your wisdom on how to handle bullies. Thank You for protecting me on a daily basis and keeping me safe. I put You in remembrance of Your Word that says in Psalm 121:7-8 (NKJV) that You will preserve me and protect me from all evil. You have promised to bless my going out and coming in. Your Word says that no weapon formed against me shall prosper and that no harm shall come to me. Thank You for giving Your angels charge over me to keep me safe. In Jesus' name I pray. Amen!

DAY 6 — Pride Blocks Your Blessing

Chris loves playing basketball and other sports. He later discovered that he was also great at golf, which came naturally to him. His father and grandfather encouraged him to develop his skills and would often attend golfing outings with him. Chris' parents and family loved the Lord and often served in their church at various functions. His parents encouraged him to follow his dreams and, more importantly, to seek the Lord for direction. As Chris's skills in golf developed, he became more prideful, often being disrespectful to his father and other adults seeking to provide guidance. He would allow his pride to get in the way of the team, often lacking professional courtesy on the golf course and during tournaments. Chris was listening to the voices that were telling him how great he was, which were drowning out the voices from his parents and other godly advisors. He started discounting the instructions of seasoned golfers because he wanted to do things his way. At age 17, he thought he knew it all. Chris loved the hype he was getting from his friends and became difficult to coach. His team members would rather lose than play with him. He became increasingly more prideful, and as his pride grew so did his disrespect for his father. Chris was becoming more and more rebellious and prideful.

Chris's coach scheduled a meeting with him, and Chris thought that he was going to be named lead for his team.

However, he was shocked when the coach informed him that he was being placed on probation and would miss the next three golf tournaments due to his behavior. If no improvement was noticed, he would be removed from the team. This was a serious blow to Chris's ego, and his response was to ask his parents if he could change schools rather than seek God's guidance for addressing his prideful ways. Chris' parent tried to counsel him about his prideful behavior and asked him to see a Christian counselor who was recommended by their pastor. Chris's response was that he was not mentally sick and did not need to see a counselor. Chris was convinced in his mind that his coach and team members were jealous and envious of his talent and this was the reason why he was being placed on probation. James, a close friend since elementary school and a team member, stopped by Chris' home and tried to reason with him. James shared with Chris why he thought the coach took the action that he believed was best for the team and Chris. However, Chris was so angry about the coach's decision that he was blinded and not receptive to what James was trying to share with him. Chris's rebellious behavior was drawing him away from God, his team, and his family.

In Proverbs 16:18-19 (KJV) King Solomon states:

> *"Pride goeth before destruction and a haughty spirit before a fall. Better it is to be of an humble spirit with the lowly, than to divide the spoil with the proud."*

F.O.G. Inspiration

What does Proverbs 16:18-19 teach us?

_____
_____
_____
_____

Can you think of a time when you were prideful?

_____
_____
_____
_____

What godly principles can you apply that will help you avoid a prideful spirit?

1. _____
2. _____
3. _____
4. _____
5. _____

F.O.G. Prayer

Father, I ask Your forgiveness for being prideful. My prayer is that You fill me with the knowledge of Your will for my life. Lord, the Bible says that Your Word is a lamp to my feet and a light to my path (Psalm 119:105 NKJV). I am asking that You help me to walk in a humble spirit and to give You all the glory and honor for the gifts and talents that You have blessed me with. This I pray in Jesus' name. Amen!

DAY 7 — Walking in Love

Anger can take many forms in our lives. If we don't get our way, we become upset. Your parents remind you daily of the family rules. You become upset and start to rebel when they simply remind you to keep your room clean or inquire about your homework. Your friends don't agree with you, and instead of seeking to understand their view point, you shut down and become angry with them. You focus on what they did or said and allow it to grow and fester. Proverbs 14:29 (NKJV) states: "He who is slow to wrath has great understanding, But he who is impulsive exalts folly."

Twelve-year-old James' anger issues had surfaced in the third grade. His father had received several complaints from teachers about his outbursts and behavior. James' father, a single parent, did not know how to handle the situation and thought his son would grow out of it. However, James' temper and outbursts only grew worse. The counselor at James' school recommended that his father get help for his son. He agreed to, but never did. James was aggressive with other kids during recess at school. None of the students wanted to hang out with him and his teachers received numerous complaints. James' father attended a meeting at school with James' teacher and counselor. James' father was shocked to hear how many complaints they had received about James. His teacher shared that she had difficulty getting him to be respectful in the class and received complaints from other students about his behavior daily.

James became upset with his sister when she refused to follow his instructions. He shoved her head into a wall in their home and broke her front teeth. James' father was now being forced to see the impact of his son's pent-up anger, which James had been taking out on others around him for years. Instead of accepting responsibility for his actions and the harm he had inflicted on his sister, James' response was that this was the way he was wired. Now his father was forced to get the help for James and his family that they needed. James' sister was afraid of him and told their father that she did not feel safe around him.

F.O.G. Inspiration

In Proverbs 15:1-2 (KJV) King Solomon said:

"A soft answer turneth away wrath: but grievous words stir up anger. The tongue of the wise useth knowledge aright: but the mouth of fools poureth out foolishness."

Daily you will have the opportunity to display anger or walk in love. Take time to mediate on the above scriptures and focus on the benefits of walking in love versus demonstrating anger. How can you honor God by walking in love?

After mediating on the following verse:

Ecclesiastes 7:9 (NKJV)

> *"Do not hasten in your spirit to be angry, for anger rests in the bosom of fools."*

answer the questions below.

How do you handle anger or being upset with someone?
_____
_____
_____
_____

Based on guidance from the Bible, what are three (3) principles you can use to walk in love and control your anger?
1. _____
2. _____
3. _____

Did you know that anger kept Moses out of the Promised Land? Read Numbers 20:12. Moses was greatly used by God; he parted the Red Sea, brought water forth from a rock, and God gave Moses the Ten Commandments. He was hand chosen by God to lead His people out of Egypt. But Moses was not allowed to enter the Promised Land. God told Moses to speak to the rock and in anger Moses struck the rock.

— F.O.G. | FOCUS ON GOD —

What does Proverbs 29:22 say about an angry man or woman?

_____
_____
_____
_____

F.O.G. Prayer

Father, I seek Your help in dealing with my anger. I want to walk in love and ask for Your help in controlling my anger. I admit that I need Your help. I receive Your strength and power to help me walk in joy, peace, and love. In Jesus' name I ask. Amen!

— PART 2 —
Developing Godly Relationships

In order to develop godly relationships, you need God's wisdom. In Proverbs 4:7 (NKJV) King Solomon states: "Wisdom is the principal thing; therefore get wisdom. And in all your getting, get understanding." We need to *Focus on God* for His wisdom in developing healthy godly relationships. How do you choose friends or business associates? What filters do you use to develop godly relationships? In Psalm 32:8, David says the Lord will instruct you and teach you in the way you should go; God has promised to guide us with His eye.

DAY 8 — Developing Relationships that Honor God

Do your friends add value to your life or do they drain you? In Proverbs 12:26 (NKJV) King Solomon said:

> *"A righteous man is cautious in friendship, But the way of the wicked leads them astray."*

Robbie began hanging out with the cool kids at school. At first they made fun of him because he was smart and a member of the Honor Society. Chris, the leader of the group, had informed Robbie that he had to do Chris' homework and threatened him if he didn't. Robbie, desiring to shed himself of his nerd image, not only took care of Chris' homework, but began to hang out with the group. Chris and his friends were known around the school for bullying, stealing, and selling drugs. They became Robbie's protection and he enjoyed the attention that he received from hanging out with Chris and his posse. First Chris exposed Robbie to marijuana, and later to various forms of hard drugs. Robbie's parents noticed the difference in his behavior and received complaints about his behavior from his school. Because Robbie's parents were experiencing marital problems they failed to get Robbie the help he needed. His siblings were also of no help due to their own struggles with drugs and alcohol.

Robbie became increasingly more rebellious as his drug use increased. He started cursing, staying out late, and was arrested for shoplifting. He also had started to dress differently: black saggy pants, black t-shirts with crossbones and skulls. After Robbie got arrested for shoplifting, he tried calling Chris for help but Chris refused and told him he was on his own. The police contacted his parents and his dad bailed him out. Robbie did not seem remorseful as he sat in the back of his parents' car. Robbie was surprised when they arrived at their home and his parents prayed with him. They told him that he had to apologize to the store owner and enroll in a treatment program. Robbie shared with his parents that he was only trying to fit in at school, but it resulted in bad decisions. He also felt lost with no one to talk with because his home was a war zone and everyone was escaping in some form. He thought the gang at school was his way out and his new family. This led to several bad choices.

What qualities do you look for when you are choosing a friend? God is concerned about you and wants to bless you with godly friends. You can pray and ask God to bless you with the right friends and to remove all ungodly influences from your life. When you F.O.G., He will give you wisdom for selecting godly friends.

Proverbs 13:20 (NKJV) states:

> *"He that walketh with wise men shall be wise; but a companion of fools shall be destroyed."*

The Word of God provides guidance for developing godly relationships.

F.O.G. Inspiration

Take time to examine your close friendships. Do they honor your relationship with God? Are they drawing you closer to God or are they drawing you into the world?

_____
_____
_____
_____

During your examination of your friends, do they support your moral values? How would you complete this sentence?

My close friends:

_____
_____
_____
_____

If you invited them to church would they attend? Your friends may be good people, but are they leading you away from the Lord? Are your friends encouraging you to do or say things or engage in activities you know do not honor your Christian values?

— F.O.G. | FOCUS ON GOD —

After reading Proverbs 13:20, how should you respond to pressure from your friends?

_____
_____
_____
_____

List three (3) things that you commit to do over the next 21 days to eliminate any ungodly relationships in your life:
1. _____
2. _____
3. _____

F.O.G. Prayer

Father, I ask that You surround me with godly friends and thank You for the removal of all ungodly influences in my life. I ask You to strengthen me and give me wisdom to eliminate all ungodly influences. In Jesus' name I pray. Amen!

DAY 9 — Addressing Moral Impurity

In 2 Timothy 2:22 (NKJV) the Apostle Paul writes:

> *"So flee youthful passions and pursue righteousness, faith, love, and peace, along with those who call on the Lord from a pure heart."*

The world we live in today is very different from the one your parents grew up in. This new technology age is wonderful; however, it can also expose you to many ungodly things. With the touch of your mouse you may find yourself exploring websites that don't honor your relationship with God. Your friends may tell you that it's okay and just a part of finding yourself or growing up. Some may say that everyone does it at least once and it's okay or what is the harm in just looking at it.

Pornography is a billion-dollar industry, and manufacturers target the young and innocent. Satan's plan is to draw you into his nest of sexual vices and get you stuck at an early age.

Let me share a story about Abby. Abby is a 15-year-old honor student and loves the Lord. She is not very popular at school, but all her teachers admire her because she is talented and respectful of those in authority. Abby is very attractive but does not feel attractive because she is very insecure about her appearance. She doesn't wear any make up except for lip gloss and dresses very modestly. Joseph is 16 and attends the same school as Abby. Joseph plays football and is very popular. All the girls at their school want to be seen with him. Abby is asked to tutor Joseph because he is failing several classes. Joseph lives for sports and does not study and has been placed on academic probation until his grades improve.

All the girls in Abby's class told her how honored she should be to tutor Joseph. They would give anything to spend that much time alone with him.

During the tutoring sessions Joseph, because of a bet with his jock friends, starts playing on Abby insecurities. At each session Joseph would flirt with Abby and exposed Abby to sexually explicit pictures on his cell phone and pressure Abby to loosen up and relax. Joseph convinced Abby that this was the norm and that all the students were engaging in some type of sexual behavior. During the study sessions, Joseph became more aggressive in seducing Abby, telling her how beautiful she was and that she was special to him. His behavior led to inappropriate touching and later to sexual sin. Abby sensed within her spirit that what Joseph was suggesting and his advances were not in line with her moral values. Abby, during each session, was being deceived by Joseph's behavior. Abby gave in to the seductive pressure instead of fleeing from his advances. Joseph shared his conquest with his buddies and pictures he had taken of them without Abby's knowledge. Abby found out and became depressed and was ashamed of her behavior. Her grades and her relationship with God suffered; she felt dirty and unworthy to pray and attend church. Joseph simply moved on to his next victim at school after telling everyone about his conquest of Abby. When Joseph saw Abby at school, he would just smile and walk past her as if nothing had happened. The above scene is played out daily in schools and on college campuses around the world.

Abby's parents prayed with her and told her how much she was loved by them and Jesus. They daily encouraged Abby to focus on her future and the promises in God's Word. Abby's parents helped her face this challenge and find her way back to Jesus by spending time focusing on the Word of God and meditating on His plan and purpose for her life. It took several months, but Abby eventually realized how much God loved her and that she was forgiven.

Nearly a quarter of teenagers said they have viewed pornography or sex at school, according to a report released January 10, 2023 by Common Sense Media, a nonprofit that studies the impact of technology on youth.

F.O.G. Inspiration

What should Abby have done to prevent being taken advantage of by Joseph?

_____
_____
_____
_____

What steps can you take to overcome the weaknesses of the flesh? Read Romans 6:12-13. What does it state that you should do with your body?

_____
_____
_____
_____

— F.O.G. | FOCUS ON GOD —

"Flee from sexual immorality. Every other sin a person commits is outside the body, but the sexually immoral person sins against his own body" 1 Corinthians 6:18 (NKJV).

List at least three (3) steps you can take to refrain from viewing and listening to sexually suggestive material, games, shows, or songs.

1. _____
2. _____
3. _____

F.O.G. Prayer

Father, I seek Your will in helping me to honor my commitment to stay pure and free of any moral impurities. I offer myself to You. I commit to live a life of purity and to honor You in all that I do. In Jesus' name I pray. Amen!

DAY 10 — Movies, Music, and Messages

This generation is dependent on technology. How do you determine which movies you will see or what music you will listen to? What are you allowing access to? Is it feeding your spirit or eroding your walk with God? Often we accept what is the norm, though it does not support our Christian beliefs, yet is politically accepted by society. Music and movies have become increasingly anti-Christian and more accepting of "anything goes." Teens and young adults are encouraged to explore their sexual desires and identity issues at an early age. Society is telling us that it's okay to be sexually active and that this is the new norm. The result of this new freedom is an increase in sexually transmitted diseases, increased teen pregnancy, and sexual identity confusion.

Nicole was excited about entering high school and the new adventures she thought it would bring. Nicole had lived a sheltered life. Her parents were very protective and she was raised in a godly home. No area of Nicole's life was off limit to her parents. They monitored her social media accounts [e.g. internet access, Facebook account, and cell phones]. Nicole was constantly teased by some of the girls at school because of her conservative views and professed love for God. Several of Nicole's friends on the soccer team encouraged her, contrary to her parents' rules, to dress differently or more freely. She gave in to the peer pressure from her team members. Nicole started wearing make-up and dressing in a more revealing way—showing more "skin," as her friends encouraged her. She would hide clothing and make-up in her locker at school and change after she arrived. Nicole liked the attention these changes brought her and she started hanging out with a popular group at school. Her choice in music drastically changed. She was now being exposed to music her parents had forbidden her to listen to and movies that she was forbidden from seeing. Nicole became rebellious and starting making arrangements to attend team parties that her parents were against. At the parties everyone was encouraged to drink alcohol, experiment with drugs and experiment with sexual encounters.

Nicole wanted to fit in so she decided that she would only go so far and would not drink anything other than sodas or punch. What Nicole did not know was the punch was spiked with drugs. She did not know how she got home or what had happened at the party. Nicole was in shock at what had happened and was thinking that she could put all of this behind her without her parents finding out what she had done. Nicole did not realize that her friends had been posting pictures of her on their Facebook page, which revealed some of their sexual exploits she had been hiding from her parents. She thought the pics were just fun and would not be shared with others outside of the group.

Recent studies reveal that pre-teens to young adults spend more than 7.0 hours a day on various forms of social media [e.g. T.V., music, surfing the internet, or other social networking]. Most social media and other media forms promote anti-Christian values. Two out of three shows give explicit sexual content. She noticed that she was receiving pock-ups on her phone to illicit sites that she had not logged onto.

— GAIL CHARLES WRIGHT —

F.O.G. Inspiration

In Romans 12:1-2 (New King James Version) the Apostle writes:

> *"I beseech you therefore, brethren, by the mercies of God, that you present your bodies a living sacrifice, holy, acceptable to God, which is your reasonable service. And do not be conformed to this world, but be transformed by the renewing of your mind, that you may prove what is that good and acceptable and perfect will of God."*

After reading the above scriptures, list ways that you can present your body as a living sacrifice, holy and acceptable to God.

1. _____
2. _____
3. _____

Why do you think the Lord wants us to remain pure and not engage in sex outside of traditional marriage?
_____
_____
_____
_____

— F.O.G. | FOCUS ON GOD —

F.O.G. Prayer

Write a prayer asking God to help you present your body as a living sacrifice and to help you renew your mind, focusing on Him.

_____
_____
_____
_____

Father, I ask for the right friends and thank You for removing all ungodly influences from my life. You have promised that when I delight myself in You and seek Your face that everything my hand touches shall prosper. I speak these promises over my life and receive them today in Jesus' name. Amen!

DAY 11 — Eliminating Bitterness and Strife

    Maxine's parents were divorced and she was never able to spend any time with her father. Maxine longed for a closer relationship with Dad. She often wondered why he never tried to spend any time with her. Maxine's dad had remarried and spent most of his time with his new family. Because of the expenses of supporting a new family, Maxine's dad stopped supporting her financially. Maxine constantly overheard her mom talking on the phone to some of her friends about Maxine's dad and how he did not support her financially and never tried to attend any of her school activities. Maxine, because of the conversations that she overheard about her dad, became extremely bitter and did not want to have anything to do with him. When Maxine's dad called her she was always very disrespectful and hung up on him. Maxine's mom never tried to correct her behavior because she was bitter herself and did not realize how her actions were wrongfully influencing her daughter's behavior toward her father and men in general. Maxine shared with her grandmother that as soon as she turned 18 she was going to change her last name because she did not want to be labeled with her dad's last name. Maxine's grandmother shared with her that God has promised to be a Father to the fatherless and would always take care of her. Maxine's grandmother encouraged her to pray for her father and prayed that God would bring healing to their relationship. Maxine would often spend summer vacation with her grandparents and they made sure Maxine spent time with her dad and especially to call her dad on Father's Day. Maxine was encouraged to honor her father and allow God to judge him, not her or her mom. She was being taught to forgive and to allow the Lord to help her.

In Ephesians 4:31 (NKJV) the Apostle Paul challenges us to:

"Let all bitterness, wrath, anger, clamor, and evil speaking be put away from you, with all malice."

We will not be able to live a life free of conflict; however, God is always with us to help us handle the conflict in a godly manner.

F.O.G. Inspiration

Are you harboring any bitterness against anyone? If so, list three (3) steps you can take to avoid bitterness.

1. _____
2. _____
3. _____

When we don't address hurt in our lives, anger and bitterness will grow, spread, and consume us. When we are angry or bitter toward someone, our Heavenly Father wants us to resolve the conflict as soon as possible. Our Father wants us to be reconciled with others even when it's not our fault. Read Matthew 5:9. How can you be a peacemaker in reconciling with someone that has offended you or a parent who neglected you?

_____
_____
_____
_____

Why is it important to eliminate bitterness from your life?

_____
_____
_____
_____

F.O.G. Prayer

Dear Lord, give me grace to work through bitterness and anger towards anyone. With Your help and guidance I know that I will be able to resolve all areas of conflicts in my life. I ask for Your help as I seek to walk in love and for the removal of all bitterness in my life. In Jesus' name I pray! Amen and Amen!

DAY 12 — Write the Vision: Developing Godly Plans

Habakkuk 2:2 (NKJV) states:

Then the Lord answered me and said: "Write the vision And make it plain on tablets, That he may run who reads it."

Write the vision and make it plain. God has great plans for us and only wants to bless us. We must seek His guidance for what He will have us to do. The norm has been for us to develop our career or life plans and ask God to bless it. Do you have a plan for your life? What are your goals for the next five (5) or ten (10) years? God wants to challenge us to dream God-sized dreams and put Him to test for helping us make them a reality!

Jill knew that she would go to college after graduating from high school. Her focus was on the worldly things that a college education would afford her. Although she was Christian, she did not seek God's plan for her life. She daily dreamed of what she would do after she graduated from high school. Her high school counselors told her that her best plan for success was to attend college and get a good job at a large corporation that offered good health benefits. Jill loved reading and actually enjoyed studying so it was no surprise that she graduated from high school with honors.

She started applying for different colleges and wanted to go as far away from home as she could. Jill's mother asked her if she had prayed about where to attend college and what God's plans were for her. Jill lied to her mother and said that she was seeking God's guidance for her future, which was totally untrue. Jill accepted a scholarship to a college that she thought would position her to get a good job and support herself. While attending college, Jill was constantly being influenced by worldly advisors and friends who did not love the Lord.

After graduating from college, Jill decided to continue her education and attend law school. Her choice was driven by the potential income she could earn as an attorney. She convinced herself that this would allow her to help her parents financially. Jill was raised in the church and loved the Lord, but she did not have a close relationship with Him. She attended a local church near college every chance she could when it did not interfere with her studies and social plans on the weekend.

Jill, like so many of us, developed plans for her future and never consulted God about it until after she ran into roadblocks. When Jill needed money for tuition and books, she prayed. When she was weary of eating ramen noodles for the sixth time in a week, she would cry out to God for help. After graduating from law school, Jill began to climb the corporate ladder and seek praise from the world. She moved from the West Coast to the East Coast, seeking money and corporate goals. Unfortunately, she never prayed about any relocation or any job offer. She used worldly factors in deciding whether to accept a new job: how much did the position pay, what benefits were linked with the position, and if the position offered an opportunity for future advancement or senior management. What looked or appeared great on paper does not necessarily end up being the best for you. Jill accepted what appeared to be a "dream job" and, after relocating for the job, soon learned that several other potential candidates had turned the job down. Her new boss was very controlling and had a reputation in the transportation industry of not allowing his direct reports to manage their teams. Jill found herself dreading getting up in the morning and feeling sick while at work.

We need to pray and seek God by praying in the Spirit for everything, such as what our career path is, what job to accept, and more importantly, which one to apply for. He has promised to lead and guide us. Psalm 1:6 (NKJV) states:

> *"The Lord knows the way of the righteous, but the way of the ungodly shall perish."*

We are not to seek money or titles; we are to seek the Lord and His way, to *Focus on God*.

God has great plans for us and cares about us. Don't make decisions based on money or titles. Money should not be your master. Let Jesus be your Master and Source.

In Jeremiah 29:11 (NKJV) the Prophet Jeremiah states:

> *"For I know the thoughts and plans that I have for you, says the Lord; thoughts and plans for welfare and peace, and not for evil, to give you hope in your final outcome."*

— F.O.G. | FOCUS ON GOD —

F.O.G. Inspiration

We must seek God in prayer for His plan and purpose for our lives. Invite God to lead you into His plan and purpose for your life. Are you currently using your God-given talents, gifts, skills, or resources in line with God's purpose for your life?

As you mediate on Jeremiah 29:11, ask the Lord to reveal to you His plan for your life.

What is the Lord saying to you?

_____
_____
_____
_____

What are you dreaming? How do you access the plans that God has for you? Meditate on His Word. Remember, God always honors His Word. You must trust in God's timing and not your own.

_____
_____
_____
_____

Start a Vision Board—what dreams has the Lord placed on your heart?

F.O.G. Prayer

Father, Your Word says if anyone lacks wisdom, to ask for it and it will be freely given. I ask for Your wisdom so that I may fulfill Your will and plan for my life. Thank You that the Holy Spirit will lead and guide me daily. In Jesus' name I pray. Amen!

DAY 13 — Honoring Parents

Nancy, a high school senior, could not wait to graduate. During high school, Nancy started hanging out with the wrong crowd, against the instructions of her parents.

Nancy's parents were very protective of her and her siblings. They were not allowed to hang out after school and were instructed to come straight home. Her parents insisted on meeting any friends and monitored their phone calls.

Nancy liked the attention she was getting from this popular group at school and refused to follow the guidance of her parents. She would dress very reserved as required by her parents and started leaving more fashionable clothing in her locker at school. Nancy was seeking to please her new friends and was constantly telling her parents that as soon as she graduated and turned 18 she was leaving home and moving out to live with her friends. The closer it got to graduation, the more she started talking back to her parents and making plans to leave home

Nancy started wearing revealing clothes to attract the attention of boys at school. She became very disrespectful of her parents by refusing to go to school or attend church and other family events. When questioned about her behavior, Nancy would yell at her mother and stay out late at night. Nancy's parents could not believe the change in her behavior and how disrespectful she was at home. Her parents arranged for the family to meet with a church counselor in hopes that this would help. Nancy's older siblings tried talking to her and insisted that she respect their parents and their rules. As graduation approached, Nancy became even more rebellious. After graduation, Nancy moved out to live with her friends, and within six months was asking for her parents' forgiveness and permission to move back home. The things that Nancy took for granted (having a room, food prepared each night, and new clothing when she needed it) she was now having to provide for herself. The friends from school that she was rooming with decided that she needed to move. Nancy was not working and unable to pay her share of the rent and food. Nancy asked her parents' forgiveness and shared with them how foolish she had been. She was thankful that her parents had forgiven her and allowed her to come back home.

F.O.G. Inspiration

Ephesians 6:2-3 (NKJV),

Honor your father and mother, which is the first commandment with promise: that it may be well with you and you may live long on the earth.

Why does God want us to honor our parents?
_____
_____
_____
_____

Proverbs 13:1 (KJV),

A wise son heareth his father's instruction: but a scorner heareth not rebuke.

What are some of the benefits God promises for those that honor their parents? List three (3) things that you can do over the next 21 days that will honor your parents if they are still living or their memory if they have passed:

1. _____
2. _____
3. _____

What are some of the benefits God promises for honoring our parents?

1. _____
2. _____
3. _____

F.O.G. Prayer

If you have done anything that dishonored your parents, ask God and your parents to forgive you.

Say this prayer:

Father, Your Word says in Ephesians 6:2-3 that we are to honor our parents so that it may be well with us. I ask Your forgiveness for not honoring my parents and ask that You help me to daily honor them. Thank You, Lord, for my parents and for the guidance and wisdom they share with me on a daily basis. In Jesus' name I pray. Amen!

DAY 14 — Honoring Those in Authority

God requires that we honor those in authority over us. This authority may come in the form of your teacher, boss, coach, or civil leader. Sometimes it is challenging to honor those in authority when they are not honorable in their behavior. When we focus on God, His Word gives us guidance on how to handle these situations in life.

Nicole was very excited about making the junior varsity basketball team at her new school. Nicole, prior to the start of the season, practiced daily to make sure she was ready. As the newest member of the team, Nicole was learning that talent and skill only took you so far. Coach Smith had her favorites and unfortunately, Nicole was not one of them. Nicole discovered that the rules were not always fairly enforced. Margo, Coach Smith's favorite player was late for practice and had been suspended from school, which according to the rules issued by Coach Smith should have been an automatic two game suspension. However, Nicole soon learned that the coach did not apply the rules as evenly as she should have. Nicole was late for practice due to a traffic accident and Coach Smith suspended her. Nicole tried to explain what happened, but the coach said that she did not want to hear it. When Nicole's mother contacted the coach and asked her why she had not suspended Margo, she became very defensive and angry. Nicole accepted the suspension and the other team players did not understand why the Coach would not allow Nicole to play. Nicole decided that she was not going to be offended by the Coach Smith's decision to suspend her. So she prayed that the Lord would help her to forgive Coach Smith for what she did. In the locker room the players distanced themselves from Margo and told her that she should have been suspended just like Nicole. Margo stated that she was special and that was why Coach Smith would not suspend her. Nicole and several of the other team players decided after the season they would no longer play for Coach Smith. They finished out the season and told the coach that they would not play next season. Nicole transferred to new school and was asked by the new coach to play on her team.

Nicole learned that you may not be treated fairly by those in authority; however, that does not give you the right to be angry and hold on to the offense. Give it to the Lord and ask for His help on how to handle it. God will help us to forgive others who have offended us.

F.O.G. Inspiration

In 1 Timothy 6:1 (NKJV) the Apostle Paul states:

"Let as many bondservants as are under the yoke count their own masters worthy of all honors, that the Name of God and His doctrine be not blasphemed."

Mediate on the above verse. Does God want us to honor an ungodly person in authority over us that mistreats us?

— GAIL CHARLES WRIGHT —

F.O.G. Prayer

Father, please forgive me for not walking in love and honoring those in authority over me. Thank You, Father, for helping me to walk in love and that I may bring glory to Your name. In Jesus' name I pray. Amen!

— PART 3 —
God's Purpose for Your Life

Does God have a purpose for your life? The answer is yes! The Bible tells us in Psalm 139:13-16 (NKJV) that God knew us and formed us in our mother's womb. Our Lord and Savior has designed great plans for us. Psalm 139:17 (NKJV) states:

> *"How precious also are your thoughts to me, O' God! How great is the sum of them."*

Based on the above scriptures, it sounds like God loves us, cares for us, and has great plans for us. So how do we receive all that He has planned for us? We can certainly start by studying His Word—focusing on God.

DAY 15 — Developing Your God-Given Gifts and Talents

Rose enjoyed reading and working with others. She was always organizing things and trying to make things better and more efficient at home and at work. At work Rose, was constantly volunteering for new assignments. She was gifted with organization and seeing what needed to be done to make processes more efficient. Rose worked hard, was very dependable, and advanced in the work place. At church Rose was told that she was like Joseph and had been given the gift of administration. Rose took classes and other training to help develop her skills.

Rose applied for a job as an administrative officer and was offered the position. The agency had received several regulatory audits and she was charged with developing strategies for addressing the audit findings. Rose prayed about the task and developed strategies for addressing all of the findings. She hosted training sessions with staff and appointed team leaders in departments. The CEO and the board of directors were very impressed with how Rose had resolved all the audit findings. Further, the federal agency stated during the exit conference that Rose had done an excellent job addressing their findings and putting strategies in place so quickly. Rose's fellow workers could not believe that she was able to handle the task so well and bring closure to all the audit findings.

Rumors begin to circulate that Rose would be the next CEO. However, the deputy decided that Rose need to be reassigned. The CEO decided after one year that he needed to re-structure the organization and Rose's position was eliminated. Rose was shocked by the news and wondered why this was happening to her. She had relocated to accept this position and had accomplished more than they had expected of her. Her new position was a contract employee offer with a reduction in salary and would only be offered for one year. Rose accepted the position and each day she purposed in her heart to do her best. She showed up early, went the extra mile, and also performed tasks that were not assigned to her. Several of the other team members asked her why she was doing this and she stated, "My gifts and talents come from the Lord, and I am doing this assignment as unto Him." They laughed at her and thought she was strange. At the end of the year the agency decided to extend Rose's contract; however, she felt lead to leave. Rose, during this time, had been focusing on God and seeking His will for her and what He would have her do. Rose felt within her heart that the Lord was leading her to start her own company, which offered legal and regulatory compliance services. Rose believed that Lord was guiding her steps and developed a plan for her new firm.

    The deputy officer who had encouraged the CEO to eliminate Rose's position was subsequently terminated within six months after Rose's resignation. He later called Rose and asked her for help in his lawsuit against the agency. Rose told him that she had never filed a complaint even though she had grounds; however, he could count on her to tell the truth. The deputy officer told Rose that he was shocked that she accepted his phone call because he knew that he had conspired against her. Rose told him that she had forgiven him before she separated from the company and prayed for him, the board of directors, and the CEO. Rose told him that she could not afford to be offended and not forgive because it would block the plans and blessings that God had for her.

F.O.G. Inspiration

Philippians 4:13 (NKJV) states:

> *"I can do all things through Christ who strengthens me."*

Challenges and setbacks may come, but they do not define who we are. God has a plan for our lives and He has given us gifts and talents to use for His glory. He will give us the strength and wisdom to handle the betrayals and attacks.

Recall a time when you were betrayed. How did you feel and how did you handle it?

1. _____
2. _____
3. _____

What gifts or talents has the Lord given you? Think of three (3) ways that you can use them to further the spreading of the Word.

1. _____
2. _____
3. _____

— F.O.G. | FOCUS ON GOD —

F.O.G. Prayer

Lord, thank You for choosing me before the foundations of the world. I am so grateful for the gifts and talents that You have placed inside me. I ask You to guide me and help me to develop these gifts and talents so that I may use them to advance the spreading of Your Word. I desire to help others come to know and love You as I do. In Jesus' name I pray. Amen!

DAY 16 — What Is God's Plan for Your Life?

In Psalm 32:8 (NKJV) the Word states:

"I will instruct you and teach you in the way you should go; I will guide you with my eye."

We all wonder if God has a plan for our lives. If He does, why doesn't He just reveal it to us? Let me share the story of David, a talented 6 foot 9 inch tall basketball player.

David enjoyed playing basketball and was a gifted player; he was captain of his high school team and after graduating David received a college basketball scholarship. He was excited about receiving the scholarship as he prepared to start this new phase of his life. David's parents and siblings were so proud of him because he was first son/brother to go college on a scholarship. David's parents had prayed over him and with him before he left for college. They encouraged him to take time to find a local church to attend and to read his Bible.

After arriving at college, David had to adjust to living in the dorms with two roommates and attending several classes. David's counselors offered help in getting him adjusted to being on his own and balancing attending classes, practicing, and playing college basketball. The big challenge facing David was the fact that he was not the lead on basketball team and he had to learn how to play with his other team members. The team captain welcomed David to the team and offered to practice with him, which David at first accepted and later decided that he was more skilled than the captain and did not need his coaching. David, after the first year of college, began to challenge the basketball captain's authority due to his scoring each game and being ranked high in the region for rebounds and assists. By the time David entered his junior or third year he was operating in pride. He no longer read his Bible or attended chapel service on campus. When asked by his parents if he was attending church, he simply lied to them. David loved all the attention he was getting around campus and in the local community.

The college newspaper and the local news publications were highlighting his achievements on the basketball court. Also, David was enjoying all the attention he was getting from girls at school. Based on all the press David was receiving, he decided to recommend to his basketball coach that he be named captain of the team, which the coach agreed to. David did not realize that his other team members were concerned with his leadership because he was always bragging on himself as if there were no other members of the team but him. He was creating a lot of strife.

David was so focused on his basketball career and visions of being drafted by the NBA that his grades were falling below the requirements for his basketball scholarship. David thought that because he was the lead, or in his mind the star, of the team the rules and regulations regarding scholastic achievements did not apply to him. He received notice of his academic failure and was placed on probation and given a period of time to adjust his grade point average in order to remove the probationary status. David was angry and blew up at the coach and requested that the coach correct this matter immediately if he wanted him to continue to play on the team. He was shocked when the coach informed him that he had been given several warnings that he ignored. They had arranged for tutors to help him but he never attended the sessions and failed to take the matter seriously. He was reaping the consequences of his prideful behavior. David felt the coach and his counselors had failed him and decided to drop out of college at the end of his junior year and joined the Marines. David tried to bring his same prideful behavior into the Marines, which was eliminated during the 13 weeks of Marine Corps Recruit Training; he learned to prevail. David was learning to be humble.

F.O.G. Inspiration

In the story above, David was talented but very prideful. God had given David a talent but he was not utilizing his gifts for the Lord or seeking the Lord's guidance regarding his gift or the plans God had for his life.

In James 4:6 (NKJV) the Apostle James states:

*"God resists the proud,
But gives grace to the humble."*

The Word of God states that He gives grace to the humble. Also, in verse 10 it states: He (God) will lift you up!

Meditating on the above verses, how can you resist being prideful?

_____
_____
_____
_____

— F.O.G. | FOCUS ON GOD —

Why do you think God resists the proud?

_____
_____
_____
_____

F.O.G. Prayer

If you have been prideful, write a prayer asking for God's help and guidance to remove pride and selfishness from your life.

_____
_____
_____
_____

DAY 17 — Applying God's Wisdom for Your Future

In Proverbs 3: 5-6 (New KJV) King Solomon states:

"Trust in the Lord with all your heart, and lean not on your own understanding; in all your ways acknowledge Him, and He will direct your paths."

God has promised to give us clear guidance if we only trust Him.

Megan, as a child, was always very friendly and caring of others. As she grew and entered high school she decided that she wanted to be a registered nurse. During summer vacations she volunteered at nursing homes to help the elderly. She prayed for the elderly while serving them in the nursing home. Megan would also volunteer for other hours at the nursing home to help the nurses assigned to the residents' care. After graduating from high school, Megan received a scholarship and entered a nursing program. Prior to heading off to college, Megan prayed with her parents for protection and wisdom. Her local pastor and church members prayed for Megan. Megan embraced her training as a gift from God and prayed that the Lord would lead and guide her as she embarked on this journey.

Megan excelled in her studies, and after graduating from college received several job offers from various hospitals. Megan prayed about her decision as to which job offer to accept. On paper one job offer appeared to offer all the benefits and salary that she had been praying for. Megan felt lead to accept the position and was welcomed as a new member of the nursing staff team. Megan was always trying to help not only the patients assigned to her care but also her fellow nurses. Megan, after three years on the job, decided that she would continue her education by taking specialized training in clinical skills. Megan noticed that as promotional opportunities were posted that sometimes she was not considered for an interview because Human Resources determined that she did not meet the qualifications. Megan was shocked to hear from the other nurses she worked with that other team members who had less work experience than she did received requests from Human Resources for interviews and one was actually offered the position. Megan decided that she would not be offended and prayed about how she should proceed; should she stay in the current job or start looking for another position with a larger hospital that offered more opportunities? Several of Megan's colleagues encouraged her to file a discrimination claim. However, Megan sought the counsel of godly advisors and decided that she would allow the Lord to fight her battles.

Megan decided that she would start preparing for upcoming nursing advancement as she researched the different type of positions that were being posted at various hospitals and clinics. She prayed with her parents and decided that she would fast to hear clearly from the Lord as to how to prepare for upcoming opportunities. Megan began by focusing on God and all the verses that dealt with godly wisdom. Megan knew that the Lord would always guide her and order her steps so that she could achieve the plans He had for her life. Daily, Megan asked the Lord to give her supernatural wisdom and divinely empower her with increased skill and knowledge in nursing as she serviced her patients.

Megan applied for another posted position; she was granted an interview and then offered the position. Megan was very pleased and gave thanks to Lord for preparing her and granting her favor with the interview team. During the negotiation phase for salary, Megan prayed about what she felt the Lord was guiding her to request and accept. Megan was surprised when the head of nursing stated that she could only be offered a lower percentage of increase due to budget issues. Megan prayed, and decided that she would accept the offer and perform her duties as unto the Lord.

Things were very busy at hospital and Megan decided that she would continue her nursing training and enter a graduate nurse program; she trusted that the Lord was leading and guiding her steps. Megan trusted the Lord and knew that He had great plans for her.

F.O.G. Inspiration

In Proverbs 2:4-5 (NKJV) King Solomon states:

> *Then he taught me, and he said to me, "Take hold of my words with all your heart; keep my commands, and you will live. Get wisdom, get understanding; do not forget my words or turn away from them."*

— F.O.G. | FOCUS ON GOD —

What does the above scripture mean to you?
_____
_____
_____
_____

How do you get godly wisdom?
_____
_____
_____
_____

Think of a decision that you will have to make in the future that requires clear guidance from God.
_____
_____
_____
_____

As you *Focus on God*, lean not to your own understanding; you will acknowledge Him and He has promised to direct your path.

F.O.G. Prayer

Lord, You said that we can come boldly before Your throne of grace to find help in our time of need. I am asking for wisdom and discernment in all the decisions that I will be faced with making today. You have said in Your Word of anyone who lacks wisdom can ask of You because You will give liberally. Thanking You for imparting to me Your wisdom and knowledge, in Jesus' name I pray. Amen!

DAY 18 — Choosing Godly Business Associates

James had dreams of starting his own business and decided to develop a business plan during his junior year in college. All his friends had encouraged him to venture out on his own and he felt that the time was right, given the contacts he had established and the limited capital he had reserved for his start-up. James knew he would need support for his business and struggled with which friends or colleagues he should approach to join him. Paul was aggressive and always looking for the next great venture to get involved in. However, James was concerned about Paul's ethics and lack of Christian values. Marvin- company with James and appeared to be more focused and grounded than Paul. James was torn between which friends he should select for his new business venture. If he selected Paul, he ran the risk of possibly losing Marvin as a friend. He had grown up with Marvin and had been friends with him for years. Paul was more aggressive and would be helpful in getting the business off the ground as well as being good for marketing the company. However, James was concerned about the appearance of borderline unethical tactics that Paul was known for using. Paul shared his proposal with James, which James reasoned was best for his company. James, feeling good about his decision, decided to share the news with his parents, who in turn asked if he had prayed and sought God's guidance about his decision. Was he sure that this was what God wanted him to do and who God wanted him to go into business with? James's response was that he would pray later and that he was sure God only wanted the best for him; he was not listening to what the Lord was trying to reveal to him about how he should develop and grow his business.

After agreeing to partner with Paul, James noticed that Paul's behavior changed. He was telling clients that he was the owner of the firm and that James was an associate. Paul was very prideful and would do anything to close a deal. Paul's unethical behavior alienated potential clients, who refused to do business with James. James later discovered that Paul had made promises to potential clients that James was unable to keep. Paul became hostile when questioned about his behavior and told James that he didn't need scrutiny, especially since–he thought he was an equal partner. James now realized what his parents were trying to communicate to him. He should have prayed and sought God's guidance before being influenced by his flesh and being unduly influenced by Paul.

James was correct. God does care about us and wants only the best for us. However, we must *Focus on God* and seek His guidance in all that we do. We must also trust God's timing and do not try to get ahead of God. We are warned against associating with, taking advice from, and hanging out with the ungodly. God's Word promises that we will be blessed and prosper if we *Focus on God* and mediate on His Word.

— GAIL CHARLES WRIGHT —
F.O.G. Inspiration

Psalm 1: 1-3 (KJV) states:

> *Blessed is the man that walketh not in the counsel of the ungodly, nor standeth in the way of sinners, nor sitteth in the seat of the scornful. But his delight is in the law of the Lord; and in his law shall he meditate day and night. And he shall be like a tree planted by the rivers of water, that bringth forth his fruit in his season, his leaf also shall not wither, and whatsoever he doeth shall prosper.*

Should Christians engage in business relationships with non-Christians? We must seek God's guidance in all that we do, including selecting business partners.

_____
_____
_____
_____

What does the Word of God say about those that lack wisdom? Read Proverbs 4:14. List three benefits of not walking in the counsel of the ungodly:
1. _____
2. _____
3. _____

— F.O.G. | FOCUS ON GOD —

F.O.G. Prayer

Father, I know that You care about me and I ask for Your guidance in seeking whom You will have me to enter into business relationships with. I seek to honor You in all that I do, and therefore, I pray for godly alliances and for open doors that no man can shut, as well as closed doors that no man can open. I seek Your knowledge and skill so that I may develop and grow my business in accordance with Your purpose and plan. You have promised to bless the work of my hands which I commit to You. I plead the blood of Jesus over my business and thank You for the ministering spirits that You have assigned to go forth to bring in new clients and/or customers. Thank You, Father, that You are the CEO of my business. In Jesus' Name I pray. Amen!

DAY 19 — Wisdom for Trials and Tests

Juan's family was Catholic and regularly attended Mass. Juan remembered the time that he received first communion at the age of seven and how proud his parents were of him. He had attended all the preparatory classes in his parish and his parents helped him prepare at home.

Juan, as a child, loved attending church and would help his father, who worked in their parish church as a custodian. Juan's priest had suggested to Juan's father that Juan consider serving as an altar boy. Juan continued serving and attending church until high school, when he started associating with other teens in his neighborhood and school; they did not know the Lord or attend church. They began to draw Juan away from the church. Juan was being exposed to a world outside of the church that his family had sheltered him from. His parents tried to counsel him, but Juan's new friends were telling him that he was his own man and could decide what was best for his life, not his parents or God. Juan became more rebellious the more time he spent with his new friends.

Juan's new friends were members of a local gang and welcomed him into their "family." Juan started hanging out with them and staying with them on weekends. When things got heavy, they were drinking and doing drugs. Juan was torn between engaging in this behavior and also stealing to support their habits. Juan would leave and return home when things got heated. He found relief at home.

Juan's parents were praying daily for him and asking him to stay away from these young boys. His parents read Proverbs 1:8-11 (NKJV) to him:

> *My son, hear the instruction of your father,*
> *And do not forsake the law of your mother;*
> *For they will be a graceful ornament on your head*
> *And chains about your neck.*
> *My son, if sinners entice you,*
> *Do not consent.*
> *If they say, Come with us; let us lie in wait to shed blood;*
> *Let us lurk secretly for the innocent without cause.*

Juan's parents shared with him how his behavior had changed and how he no longer wanted to attend Mass. These new friends were drawing him away from the Lord. They warned him that this would only lead to destruction. Juan became angry and shared that he was in control, that he was not engaging in any illegal activities.

In Proverbs 2: 10-13 (NKJV) King Solomon states:

> *When wisdom enters your heart, and knowledge is pleasant to your soul, discretion will preserve you; understanding will keep you, to deliver you from the way of evil, from the*

man who speaks perverse things, from those who leave the paths of uprightness to walk in the ways of darkness.

Juan daily was being led in the path of darkness. What Juan was not aware of was that his new friends had plans to rob a fast-food store and Juan was the driver of the car. Juan was not aware of what was going on inside the store. They had told Juan that they were getting some subs and it was not until after they had robbed the store and ran out, jumped into car, and ordered Juan to speed away that he understood. Juan was shocked and wanted to stop the car and run away; however, his friends told him they would kill him and he was as guilty as they were because he was driving the getaway car. What Juan did not know was that cameras outside of store had captured the car and police were tracking them. They were located and all were arrested. Juan called his parents, who arranged bail for him, and his priest made arrangements for an attorney who was a member of the church to represent him. Juan found out from his attorney that the other members of the gang were stating that Juan was aware of the robbery and volunteered to drive the car. Juan was now faced with proving his innocence.

F.O.G. Inspiration

Have you been faced with a trial at work or school? How did you handle it?

_____
_____
_____
_____

— F.O.G. | FOCUS ON GOD —

What godly principles did you use to handle the situation? Or what godly principles can you apply in the future?
1. _____
2. _____
3. _____

F.O.G. Prayer

Lord, thank You for your wisdom. Your words say that Your wisdom has entered my heart, Your knowledge is pleasant to my soul, discretion will preserve me, and Your understanding will keep me and deliver me from evil. I ask You to help me to clearly hear Your voice and thank You for preserving me from evil. Amen!

DAY 20 — Success God's Way

No child grows up and says, "I just want to get by." We all desire from an early age to be a success in life. Some of us dream of being a teacher, doctor, or a lawyer. The form of success and what it looks like may take different forms and mean different things depending on the individual.

Joshua 1:8 (NKJV) states:

> *This book of the Law shall not depart from your mouth, but you shall mediate in it day and night, that you may observe to do according to all that is written in it. For then you will make your way prosperous and then you will have good success.*

Lucy, at an early age, decided that she wanted to become a psychiatrist because she wanted to help others. She spent most of her time reading and preparing to attend college. After meeting with her high school career counselor, Lucy realized that she need to make some adjustments in her future plan because she did not think she could survive medical school. She modified her goal to become clinical psychologist.

Lucy never developed a plan for attending college; prior to graduating from high school she took the advice of her counselor and applied at several colleges and accepted what she thought was the best offer for her. Lucy's parents taught her to how to pray and they regularly attended church every Sunday. Her parents were unable to financially support her college education; however, they prayed daily for her and offered the following guidance: they encouraged Lucy to make Christian friends — friends who supported her moral values. When she found a part-time job, they told her to make sure that she honored those in authority over her, and to study and apply herself regarding her classes at college.

Lucy found a local church to attend and would regularly pray to God. She thought because she attended church and prayed that God would answer her prayers. However, she did more talking to God with a list of what she needed and wanted versus seeking God's direction for her life. Her friends at college encouraged her to skip classes and call in sick at work so she could hang out with them and attend parties and networking gatherings. Lucy's friends at college appeared to be successful and encouraged her focus on what the world considered successful: change her major from psychology to business; climbing the corporate ladder, and joining private clubs to network with others. She was encouraged to dine at restaurants that she could not afford and buy expensive clothing that her friends stated helped her dress for success.

Lucy's mom would call her every Saturday to remind her to attend church on Sunday and find out how her week was. Lucy missed several calls from her mom because she was sleeping in on Saturday after attending social events with her friends during the week. She never returned the calls to her mom because she did not want to know what she was going to say about her new behavior. She had also missed several days of work and when she showed up her supervisor informed her that she was being terminated.

Lucy thought her new friends would help her; however, they began to distance themselves from her. Lucy started feeling like her life was falling apart and decided she would seek counseling from her new pastor at church. Lucy's pastor encouraged her to call her mom, share with her what was happening, and ask her forgiveness. Her parents agreed to help with her rent and Lucy committed to spending more time with God and finding a job that would allow her to complete her education. Lucy realized that she needed to develop a close relationship with God. She was determined this time to do it God's way and trust Him to help her.

F.O.G. Inspiration

Success without God is not success. The world will offer you many versions of what they believe success is. Mediating on God's Word is spending quiet time in His presence and allowing Him to review what He has for you.

Think of three (3) ways you can spend more time listening to God and mediating on His Word.

1. _____
2. _____
3. _____

Why do you think God wants you to be prosperous and have good success?

_____
_____
_____
_____

— F.O.G. | FOCUS ON GOD —

F.O.G. Prayer

Father, please forgive me for the times that I have come before You with my list. I see in Your Word in Joshua 1:8 that You desire for me to be prosperous and have good success. I am asking that You reveal Your purpose and plan for my life. Help me to clearly hear Your voice as I mediate on Your Word. In Jesus' name I pray. Amen.

DAY 21 — Establishing a Close Relationship with God

When you spend time focusing on God, He will help you fulfill His purpose for your life. I started seeking God, and a close friend shared that she had heard that Oral Roberts had daily meditated on Psalm 23, Psalm 91, and the Lord's Prayer. Now it's been more than ten years since I have been mediating daily on Psalm 23, Psalm 91, the Lord's Prayer and I added Psalm 1.

What better way is there of drawing closer to God than daily meditating on the Psalm 91, the 23rd Psalm and the Lord's Prayer. I encourage you to mediate on all these powerful prayers three times each day; take them as medicine: morning, noon, and night. I encourage you to make this a daily habit!

Let's start with the 23rd Psalm (KJV)—The Lord is My Shepherd.

The Lord is my shepherd
I shall not want
He maketh me to lie down in green pastures:
He leadeth me beside the still waters, He restoreth my soul: he leadeth me in the paths of righteousness
For his name's sake.

F.O.G. | FOCUS ON GOD

*Yea, though I walk through the valley
of the shadow of death,
I will fear no evil: for thou are with me;
thy rod and thy staff they comfort me.
Thou preparest a table before me in the
presence of mine enemies: thou
anointest my head with oil;
my cup runneth over.
Surely goodness and mercy shall follow me
all the days of my life:
and I will dwell in the house
of the Lord forever.*

Psalm 23 reveals how much the Lord loves and cares for us. When you study Psalm 23, you become aware of fact that the Lord will provide you guidance, He will protect you—because He is our shepherd we shall never be in want or lack any good things.

Mediating on Psalm 23—what does it mean to you that He is your Shepherd?

_____
_____
_____
_____

List several of the benefits listed in Psalm 23.

_____
_____
_____
_____

What do you think it means to dwell in the house of the Lord?

_____
_____
_____
_____

We have a caring loving Father that wants only the best for us. He desires to spend more time with us. When we spend time with our Heavenly Father and seek Him, this allows us to embrace the wonderful blessings that He has stored up for us. You may be thinking, if God is really a kind, loving Father, then why doesn't He just supply my need and heal my loved ones that are sick? God is a good God and has already provided a way out or solution for you; you must seek Him and He will guide you.

Matthew 6:9-13 (KJV) states:

> After this manner, therefore pray ye:
> Our Father which are in heaven,
> Hallowed be thy name.
> Thy kingdom come.
> Thy will be done
> In earth as it is in heaven.
> Give us this day our daily bread.
> And forgive us our debts,
> As we forgive our debtors.
> And lead us not into temptation,
> But deliver us from the evil.
> ¹³For thine is the kingdom and the power and
> the glory forever. Amen.

Our Father has promised to meet our needs on a daily basis, and because He is our Shepherd you shall not want! The Lord's Prayer lists several blessings that belong to us; praying this prayer grants you access to them. So how do we obtain them? You have to ask Him. He knows what we have need of, but we must ask Him. Ask, believe you shall receive, and trust Him. Hebrews 11:1 (NKJV) tells us that faith is the substance of things hoped for, the evidence of things not seen. In Romans 12:3, the Apostle Paul tells us that God has given to everyone the measure of faith. You have been given all the faith you need; start using it!

Matthew 6:32-33 (KJV) states:

> *"Your Heavenly Father knoweth that you have need of all these things." We are to seek the Kingdom of God and His will and plan. God has promised that He will supply all we need (e.g. food, shelter, rent, home, car, clothing, etc.).*

I encourage to you daily develop your relationship with our Heavenly Father. Declare His promises and speak His Word over your life, home, and family! He wants us to be blessed in all areas of our lives. Let's start receiving what He has stored up for us!

Psalm 91

Psalm 91 is one of my favorite psalms that I mediate on daily. Early in the morning and before I go to bed I spend time mediating on Psalm 91. I encourage you to mediate on and read it in more than one biblical version (New King James, and, for example the Amplified Bible).

— GAIL CHARLES WRIGHT —

My favorite version that I want to share with is the Complete Jewish Bible (CJB), which says:

> *You who live in the shelter of Elyon,*
> *who spend your nights in the shadow of Shaddai,*
> *who say to* ADONAI, *"My refuge!*
> *My fortress!*
> *My God, in whom I trust!"* –
> *He will rescue you from the trap of the hunter and from the plague of calamities;*
> *he will cover you with his pinions,*
> *and under his wings you will find refuge;*
> *his truth is a shield and protection.*
>
> *You will not fear the terrors of night*
> *or the arrow that flies by day,*
> *or the plague that roams in the dark,*
> *or the scourge that wreaks havoc at noon.*
> *A thousand may fall at your side,*
> *ten thousand at your right hand;*
> *but it won't come near you.*
> *Only keep your eyes open,*
> *and you will see how the wicked are punished.*
>
> *For you have made* ADONAI,
> THE *Most High*
> *who is my refuge, your dwelling-place.*
> *No disaster will happens to you,*
> *no calamity will come near your tent;*

*for he will order his angels to care for you
and guard you wherever you go.
They will carry you in their hands,
So that you won't trip on a stone.
You will tread down lions and snakes,
young lions and serpents you will trample
underfoot.*

*Because he loves me, I will rescue him;
because he knows my name, I will protect
him.
He will call on me, and I will answer him.
I will be with him when he is in trouble.
I will extricate him and bring him honor.
I will satisfy him with long life
and show him my salvation.*

I like to personalize the prayer; I insert my name into it. For example:

"Because Gail loves me, I will rescue her, because Gail knows my name,

I will protect her. Gail will call on me, and I will answer her. I will be with Gail when she is in trouble. I will extricate Gail and bring Gail honor. I will satisfy Gail with long life and show Gail my salvation."

Let me share with you how the Lord recently protected me and my family from harm during a rainstorm. It started off with light rain, and within one hour the rain increased with lots of thunder. The rain grew increasing heavy, with hail the size of golf balls. I generally enjoy the rain but became alarmed at the thunder and the hail. I felt lead in my spirit to stop and pray; I went into my bedroom and knelt by my bed and prayed Psalm 91, asking the Lord to protect us. I started declaring that God was our dwelling place and our refuge. I declared that no disaster, no calamity would come near our dwelling, and ended with declaring peace over the storm. After I finished praying, I heard a loud boom; I continued to think God for protecting us. My husband told me to look out the window, it appeared that our neighbor's home was on fire. We immediately started praying for their safety and the fire department that was responding to the fire. I went outside to see if I could find our neighbors and offer to help them. They shared that lighting had struck their home; praise God it was not destroyed. We offered them a place to stay; however, they shared that they had relatives that lived nearby. They later shared that the contractor that was retained to restore their home said it would take eight months. They were thankful that their home was not completely destroyed by fire.

Every day, we pray over our home and the neighborhood; we also ask the Lord to send laborers and claim those that live in our neighborhood for the Lord. Prayer works, and He will protect us and keep us safe.

Review Psalm 91 and list some of the wonderful benefits it has for us:

_____
_____
_____
_____

— F.O.G. | FOCUS ON GOD —

Take time to personalize a section of Psalm 91:

_____
_____
_____
_____

Closing Prayer

Father, I thank You for everyone reading this devotional. I pray that You will release Your blessings upon them as they seek Your face and purpose in their hearts to draw closer to You.

I ask that You would give them strength and guide their steps. Father, release Your anointing on them and bless the work of their hands; let Your favor surround them like a shield. Pour out upon them Your stored-up blessings: release Your joy, peace, grace, health, and protection. Father, we worship You and give You all the glory and praise. Thank You that You are our loving Shepherd, that You are Abba Father!

Epilogue

I always loved reading books, and had dreams of someday writing one. I started praying about writing books and felt in my spirit that I should write about what I was seeking to do, which was spend more time with God. During my quiet time with the Lord, He gave me the title — *F.O.G.* — *Focus on God*. I had started volunteering more at my church in San Bernardino and enjoyed giving back at our community events. Also, I knew I needed to grow more spiritually and decided to establish a spiritual calendar. I started scheduling attendance at various spiritually-focused events such as Kenneth Copeland Southwest Believers Conference (Anaheim and Long Beach), Jesse Duplantis Visionary Conference, Joyce Meyers Women's Conference, John Hagee Ministries Annual Fall Feast, Kim Clement's House of Destiny Meetings, and Benny Hinn's Miracle Crusades in the Los Angeles area.

I was raised in the Church of Christ and fell in love with the Lord after learning about Him and developing a relationship with Him under the direction of Rev. Dr. Frederick K.C. Price. My faith started to grow, and I knew that I needed to get off the fence and draw closer to the Lord. During my time at Crenshaw Christian Center, I was introduced to Kenneth E. Hagin and Brother Kenneth Copeland. My spirit was connecting with everything they were teaching.

Whenever Brother Copeland was in the Los Angeles area, I arranged my schedule so that I could be in his presence and receive what he was sharing spiritually.

Getting back to writing *F.O.G.* I immediately started a journal, writing down what I thought the Lord wanted in the book, especially that it should be a devotional that would help teenagers and young adults grow spiritually. I started working on the manuscript in 2010 and unfortunately I allowed other things to take priority. I was focused on launching my new consulting business and serving as a voluntary temporary judge in San Bernardino County. In 2020, after my mother went home to be with the Lord, I was feeling lonely and sorry for myself and felt in my spirit I needed to finish *F.O.G.* and get it published.

I hope you decide to implement some of the principles and suggestions for focusing on God that I have shared in this devotional. I pray that what I have shared in the stories and about mediating on the Lord's Prayer, Psalm 23—He Is your Shepherd and Psalm 91—He is your refuge and protector will bless you and your families!

About the Author

Gail Charles Wright grew up in Southwest Louisiana; she is the seventh child out of eleven. Growing up, she was very shy and loved to read. While she thought she was just an average person, the Lord was preparing her for serving Him.

Gail is an author, speaker, entrepreneur, and a licensed attorney. She has a passion for praying for and helping people succeed in life, especially in seeking the Lord. The Lord has used Gail to speak into the lives of many in the marketplace as she shares the love of God.

Gail and her husband, Larry, have been married for over 27 years and are servants of the Lord, planted at Eagle Mountain International Church in Newark, Texas.

RESOURCES FOR FURTHER GROWTH AND DEVELOPMENT

Vision

Terri Savelle Foy, www.terri.com, better known as the Vision Cheerleader

Jesse Duplantis Ministries, www.jdm.org
Vision Specialist

Victory Channel—Vision, www.kcm.org
Kenneth Copeland Ministries

Pastor George Pearson, www.kcm.org
Inside the Vision with Pastor George

Business Development

Dr. Bill Winston, www.billwinston.org
Joseph Business School, Faith and the Marketplace

Fixing the Money Thing, www.garykeesee.com

Prayer of Salvation

"Dear Lord Jesus, I believe You died for me and rose again on the third day.

I believe You are the Son of God. I confess I am a sinner and that You died for my sins.

I need Your love and forgiveness. Please forgive me for all my sins.

I ask You to come into my heart and be my Savior and Lord of my life.

Thank You for coming into my heart and making me a child of God."

Amen

Receive the Holy Spirit

As a child of the Most High King, He wants us to walk in victory and His supernatural power. Being baptized with the Holy Spirit belongs to us. He wants us to be filled and overflowing with His Holy Spirit. I encourage you to be filled with the Holy Spirit. All you have to do is ask, believe, and receive:

Declare this prayer: "Father, I need more of You. I need Your power to dwell inside of me. I see this is a gift that You have freely given to Your children. I come boldly before Your throne and ask that You fill me with your Holy Spirit. By faith in Your Word, I believe I will receive it right now. I receive it right now. I expect to speak in other tongues as Your Spirit gives me utterance. Thank You for baptizing me with the Holy Spirit!"

www.ingramcontent.com/pod-product-compliance
Lightning Source LLC
LaVergne TN
LVHW010927160125
801236LV00020B/795